Nighttime for Prosperity

Wisdom for Creating Prosperous Vibes While You Sleep

By

BRENDA LYNN JACOBSON
Foreword by AliNICOLE WOW!

Copyright © 2022 Brenda Jacobson

All rights reserved.

ISBN: 9798828451159

You may not use or reproduce by any means including graphic, electronic, or mechanical, photocopying, recording, taping, or by any information storage retrieval system without the written permission of the publisher. The only exception is using brief quotations embodied in critical articles or reviews.

DEDICATION

To all my family, friends, coaches, healers, and guides who supported me along my journey of awakening. I'm profoundly grateful for your wisdom, encouragement, and the lessons you have taught me along the way.

. . .

ACKNOWLEDGMENTS

This book is presented with enormous gratitude to my fabulous coach and mentor of all things, AliNICOLE WOW! She truly does do it all. This book is the result of her continued guidance, support, and patience.

...

FOREWORD

Vibrationally Aligning My Evening for Prosperity

Foreword by AliNICOLE WOW!

The power of vibrational alignment trumps everything and leveraging this core element for prosperity in the evening really sets the tone for not only pleasant dreams, but also quantum manifestations in your awakened reality. Having the right vibes are vital to your overall success for well-being. You're responsible for discovering your unique vibrational alignment for prosperity and this publication invites you into an intentional experience that will help you to activate more of your prosperity birthright.

One of my favorite activities to take others through in my own work in this area is creating a statement of intent for vibrational alignment followed by a song of intent and then spending time being present with the energy of prosperity. I believe starting your experience with this exercise will help you to maximize the benefits found in this resource.

I invite you to take a deep breath and make this statement of intent:

"I AM Vibrationally Aligning My Nighttime for Prosperity."

Next, I invite you to pull up a YouTube video of the Prosperity Chant by Karen Drucker. This is a great way to commune with the energy of prosperity and align with your highest intent for manifesting your divine desires.

Here are a few lyrics to the chorus of the song.

> *What do I want?*
>
> *What do I desire?*
>
> *What will bring me to my highest good?*
>
> *Prosperity, (Prosperity), I claim it (I claim it) abundance, it is mine.*

Prosperity is your birthright to claim and as you're winding down your evening and set to retire from the day. You need to lean/rest into your inheritance so that you expand and anchor your core desires at a much deeper level. Knowing what you want and desire is important however, staying open for expanded awareness around your longings will divinely align you with what will be for your highest and best potential in the present/*NOW* as well as the emerging future.

Nighttime Nuggets of Prosperity provides an experience that brings you into a new encounter of evolving your prosperity alignment as you rest into the richness of the abundance that is *YOU*! This is your core truth. You're here to be a symbol of prosperity to others. For you to fulfill this divine assignment, you must "prime" and prepare yourself in the most prosperous way so that you can authentically share and demonstrate your prosperous life from a place of *TRUTH*!

Brenda takes you on a new enchanted adventure with prosperity and provides an experience that allows you to customize your alignment to create your life from the most prosperous version of yourself at each new phase of the journey. It's time to open the treasure chest of your inner prosperity and leverage each nugget of wisdom for your highest levels of holistic success.

Repeat:

"I AM Now Vibrationally Aligned with My True Prosperous Self."

Enjoy the Continuation of Your Prosperity Journey!!!!!!!!!

Brenda Lynn Jacobson

. . .

Copyright Brenda Lynn Jacobson 2023

INTRODUCTION

The world has now transitioned from the dense, restrictive vibrations of the past into the fresh, accelerated energy of the NOW—a space I lovingly call the *Feminine Quantum*. This new energy invites you into a higher state of intuitive alignment, abundance, and ease, allowing your deepest desires to manifest effortlessly and swiftly if you are open to receiving them.

The Feminine Quantum is the untapped field of intuitive power, energetic alignment, and heart-centered leadership that lives within every woman. It's not about doing more—it's about accessing the vibrational intelligence beneath the surface. It's the space where intuition meets strategy, softness becomes strength, and your inner frequency shapes your outer reality.

This is where you stop leading from burnout, control, or competition—and start creating from wholeness, embodiment, and resonance. When you awaken your *Feminine Quantum*, you don't just shift your mindset…

- You shift your energy.
- You amplify your presence.
- You magnetize aligned opportunities.

It's not just personal growth—it's a quantum leap into your highest expression.

In the Feminine Quantum, you shift from a reality defined by force, effort, and struggle to one characterized by intuitive guidance, synchronicity, and graceful flow.

You may have noticed traditional methods of goal setting and achievement feel increasingly exhausting and ineffective. Tasks, once straightforward, now seem heavy, cumbersome, and slow. This isn't a flaw or a failure—it's an invitation. It's your inner being guiding you to let go of outdated ways and embrace a more intuitive, vibrational approach to creation, bringing a sense of liberation and relief.

Consider how effortlessly nature flourishes—flowers bloom without struggle, rivers flow without forcing their paths, and the sun rises and sets in perfect harmony. Nature intuitively knows how to align with universal energies, and so do you. The *Feminine Quantum* mirrors this natural alignment, encouraging you to tap into your innate wisdom and allow abundance to come to you with ease.

As you enter the *Feminine Quantum*, outdated strategies built on struggle, force, and linear thinking lose effectiveness. Just as creating a magnificent new recipe requires fresh ingredients, embracing this vibrant energy demands new practices and a deeper understanding of your inherent power as a creator.

Science states that people have 60,000 to 70,000 thoughts every day, and astonishingly, 90% of these thoughts are the same ones they had yesterday, the day before, and the day before that. These repetitive thoughts trigger familiar emotions, leading to predictable actions and behaviors. Actions shape our relationships, and ultimately, these relationships define our reality and identity. This cycle explains why many people find it so challenging to create lasting changes.

In the *Feminine Quantum*, you have the unique opportunity to reorganize repetitive, chaotic thoughts into harmonious, high-vibration frequencies. By consciously choosing high-frequency thoughts, you trigger expanding emotions, leading to authentic, aligned actions. These new actions reshape your relationships and redefine your world, elevating the best aspects of your past selves while illuminating them with fresh, vibrant possibilities.

Imagine what life would look like if you fully embraced this *Quantum Feminine* energy. You would wake up feeling refreshed, clear, and inspired. Opportunities you once chased now effortlessly find their way to you. Relationships would deepen, work would become meaningful, and creativity would flow abundantly. Instead of feeling overwhelmed by endless to-do lists, you would feel energized by the clarity of your vision and the ease of its fulfillment.

The essence of the *Feminine Quantum* lies in recognizing yourself and your reality as purely vibrational. Every thought, emotion, and belief carries a specific frequency, directly impacting the experiences and opportunities you attract. Your emotional states influence every cell in your body, shaping your reality from within. Elevating your vibration becomes your most essential practice, guiding you toward the life of abundance and prosperity that is your birthright.

Consider your thoughts as magnets, attracting experiences of matching vibration. Negative thoughts of scarcity, doubt, or unworthiness attract circumstances reflecting those energies. Conversely, thoughts of joy, gratitude, abundance, and confidence effortlessly attract aligned experiences and opportunities. Your thoughts and emotions are not passive—they are active creators of your reality.

Are you ready to release old identities and beliefs that no longer serve you? Are you prepared to embrace your *Feminine Quantum* and live as the highest expression of yourself? The process begins with awareness and conscious intention. It requires releasing the patterns of struggle and shifting your focus to feeling good, joyful, and abundant, regardless of your circumstances.

Nighttime is especially powerful in this process of quantum creation. It's when your conscious mind rests and your subconscious becomes active, unhindered, and profoundly receptive. This book, "*Nighttime Nuggets for Prosperity*", offers simple yet potent affirmations and prompts explicitly designed to engage your subconscious mind. Each night's reflection effortlessly aligns your energy with abundance, guiding you to intuitively attract prosperity and vibrant opportunities into your life.

Picture your subconscious mind as your most dedicated and powerful ally, tirelessly working behind the scenes to bring your desires into reality.

By providing your subconscious with clear, positive messages each night, you supercharge your ability to manifest. These nightly routines help rewrite limiting beliefs and old stories, installing empowering new programs in your neural pathways. They help you move beyond your past self and step powerfully into the identity you've created for the future.

Trust the wisdom within these pages, the process, and, most importantly, the power of your *Feminine Quantum*. Dedicating just a few minutes each night to this practice will activate profound shifts, and magnetize prosperity, ease, and fulfillment into every aspect of your experience.

Welcome to the extraordinary life you were always meant to live.

Enjoy this journey into your limitless potential.

Here's what you do each night before bed. . .

- Before you settle into bed, sit for a few minutes with this book in hand, to align your energy with the vibration of its power.

- Take several deep breaths—right down into your belly. Feel your belly expand as the air enters.

- With each exhale, allow every cell in your body to release the stress and tension it's carrying.

- Feel your body relax.

- After several deep belly breaths, bring to mind an image of what prosperity looks and feels like for you at this time.

- Sit with this image for a few more deep belly breaths.

- When it feels right to do so, open the book to a random page and read the question or statement written on it.

- Repeat this caption several times—taking a deep breath afterward each repetition.

- Imagine breathing this question or statement deep into your body.

- Release the book and allow the thought to settle into your subconscious mind.

- Sit for a few more moments until it feels right to get up.

- Settle into bed for the night and allow your subconscious to go to work making this phrase a part of your reality.

Whether it's a statement or a question it ignites your subconscious mind to make this part of your reality. As the faithful servant that it is, the subconscious will work throughout the night to discover all the ways this question or statement is true.

In the morning, take a few to follow the routine below and lock in all the hard work done by your subconscious while you slept.

Here's what you do each morning. . .

In the morning, before your day begins, take a few moments to journal your thoughts on the pages provided below each question or statement. Become aware of. . .

- What came up in your dreamscape?
- How can you answer this question or embrace this statement as your truth?
- How will this thought accelerate the flow of prosperity in your life?

Enjoy this process of evolving into the accelerated flow of the NOW energy.

> # REMEMBER, THE SECRET TO THIS BOOK IS:
>
> YOUR SUBCONSCIOUS MIND IS TASKED WITH FINDING THE ANSWERS OR PROOF FOR THESE QUESTIONS AND STATEMENTS.
>
> DO NOT ALLOW YOUR CONSCIOUS MIND TO DISCOUNT ANY OF THESE BECAUSE YOU CAN'T CURRENTLY ANSWER THEM OR BELIEVE THEM TO BE TRUE.

Here we go. . .

How can I freely attract money with my abundant thoughts?

More notes. . .

In what ways is my life already rich?

More notes. . .

I give and receive freely.

More notes. . .

My mind is open to possibilities and opportunities.

More notes. . .

How does my passion fuel my engine of creation?

More notes. . .

How am I achieving my dreams right now?

More notes. . .

How are wonders and miracles showing up
in my life?

More notes. . .

In what ways am I experiencing prosperity NOW?

More notes. . .

My perfect life already exists.

More notes. . .

What am I grateful for in my life now?

More notes. . .

How do my thoughts drive my emotions and create my world?

More notes. . .

What makes me feel the most vibrant and energetic?

More notes. . .

I am grateful for ME—the choices I make and the actions I take.

More notes. . .

How am I enjoying my path to abundance?

More notes. . .

My vulnerability is my power.

More notes. . .

What are examples of prosperity that already exists in my life?

More notes. . .

What would it take for me to prepare to improve my life NOW?

More notes. . .

Potential exists in everything.

More notes. . .

How can I adjust my thoughts to create mental prosperity?

More notes. . .

What is the vision for my life that I believe in?

More notes. . .

How is wealth pouring into my life now?

More notes. . .

How does my abundance of relationships show up in my life?

More notes. . .

How is my life growing with ease and grace?

More notes. . .

What thoughts allow me to feel satisfied
with my life?

More notes. . .

How am I shifting my habits to transform my life?

More notes. . .

What prosperity do I experience in my relationships?

More notes. . .

What do I appreciate about my life and the people in it?

More notes. . .

How am I allowing abundance into my life each day?

More notes. . .

How do I show gratitude for the abundant
flow of things in my life?

More notes. . .

I am ready to start living my magic.

More notes. . .

What thoughts encourage me to feel peaceful?

More notes. . .

The choice is always mine.

More notes. . .

What thoughts allow me to feel JOY in my life?

More notes. . .

Prosperity comes to confident people.
When do I feel confident?

More notes. . .

How can I allow myself to give and receive
in balance?

More notes. . .

What do I choose from my endless opportunities?

More notes. . .

How do I receive support from the loving people around me?

More notes. . .

I release control of my prosperity to my inner guidance.

More notes. . .

The image Source holds of me is perfection.

More notes. . .

How is the perfection of Source divinely
expressing through me?

More notes. . .

What evidence exists that positive thoughts attract a flow of prosperity into my life?

More notes. . .

What idea will I focus on to generate prosperity in my life today?

More notes. . .

How am I being proactive?

More notes. . .

The key to my evolution is building on who I already am.

More notes. . .

How is the Universe supporting me?

More notes. . .

What is the ideal life I clearly envision?

More notes. . .

There is no limit to the possibilities before me.

More notes. . .

How does the feeling of prosperity show up
in my body?

More notes. . .

This is my time of awakening to the new world.

More notes. . .

How do I experience prosperity wherever I turn?

More notes. . .

Where does the feeling of love show up in my life?

More notes. . .

Who will I share my abundance with?

More notes. . .

It is safe to let go.

More notes. . .

It's time to POWER UP! What does that mean to me?

More notes. . .

How do I feel lifeforce energy from the earth and universe revitalizing my life?

More notes. . .

How am I standing as an example of abundance?

More notes. . .

My mind is open to new ideas.

More notes. . .

How will I spread prosperity throughout my community?

More notes. . .

How does magic appear in my life?

More notes. . .

LIFE IS FUN! How does that show up for me?

More notes. . .

I hold a clear picture of my prosperous life.

More notes. . .

Money is energy. How do I align with the
energy of money in my life?

More notes. . .

How do I use authenticity as my POWER?

More notes. . .

What evidence do I have that my awareness is expanding every day?

More notes. . .

What are examples of an abundance of things in my life that make me smile?

More notes. . .

What are examples of Divine inspiration flowing to me?

More notes. . .

I am focused and clear. How does this support me?

More notes. . .

My body is in perfect health and balance.
How do I visualize this in my life?

More notes. . .

What things in my life bring me an abundance of Joy.

More notes. . .

How do I control my inner experience of life?

More notes. . .

Life is easy. How is my life getting easier
each day?

More notes. . .

I am a money magnet.

More notes. . .

What possibilities exist for me when I choose to SOAR?

More notes. . .

I feel happy where I am and ready for more.

More notes. . .

I am lucky. What are 5 examples of luck showing up in my life?

More notes. . .

I create my reality. What is the reality I choose to create for myself?

More notes. . .

I deserve a harmonious and loving life.
What does this look like for me?

More notes. . .

What would it take for me to attract positive, like-minded people into my life?

More notes. . .

What strategy do I use to easily shift my energetic state?

More notes. . .

How does empathy for myself and others feel in my body?

More notes. . .

Everything I touch is a success. What are 5 examples of this?

More notes. . .

What creative ways does money flow to me?

More notes. . .

What would it take for me to embody my soul's gifts?

More notes. . .

What is the best way to connect to my inner self?

More notes. . .

I am now open to receive prosperity.

More notes. . .

What do I do to show compassion for myself?

More notes. . .

When do I most feel understood?

More notes. . .

What aspects of my life are evolving into a new dimension?

More notes. . .

What allows me to feel amazing amounts of energy?

More notes. . .

When I illuminate my inner magic what do I
see within me?

More notes. . .

I love my flow of abundance.

More notes. . .

How am I bringing great value to the world?

More notes. . .

My income increases while I sleep.

More notes. . .

How does my productivity increase when I focus on it?

More notes. . .

How do I reclaim the joy and love within me?

More notes. . .

When I release the stories that no longer
serve me what do I replace them with?

More notes. . .

What do I truly desire?

More notes. . .

Abundance and prosperity are my birthright.

More notes. . .

How do I feel like I have risen from the ashes like the Phoenix?

More notes. . .

What expanding beliefs do I now embrace?

More notes. . .

How is prosperity showing up for me now?

More notes. . .

How do I use all my talents to create abundance?

More notes. . .

What is the world my imagination creates for me?

More notes. . .

I feel blessed.

More notes. . .

What thoughts allow me to feel most abundant?

More notes. . .

I continually have new choices and options.
5 examples of these are. . .

More notes. . .

How does courage show up in my life?

More notes. . .

How do I feel knowing that I am creating a magnificent personal experience?

More notes. . .

I deserve the best and I accept it now. How does that look and feel to me now?

More notes. . .

What thoughts cause me to acceptance?

More notes. . .

What strategies am I using to elevate my vibration?

More notes. . .

I squeeze the most out of every moment.

More notes. . .

What activities allow me to expand my heart center?

More notes. . .

I feel grateful to be evolving and it is showing up in my life as. . .

More notes. . .

How do my thoughts create the feeling of trust?

More notes. . .

What are the new powers I am continually tapping into?

More notes. . .

I am infinitely abundant.

More notes. . .

When do I deliver more than expected?

More notes. . .

What is my soul's purpose that I am already living?

More notes. . .

What thoughts create optimistic feelings in me?

More notes. . .

How do I feel when I listen to positive comments of others?

More notes. . .

What are 5 ways I envision myself winning at life?

More notes. . .

I am supported by a global community.
Who is in this community now?

More notes. . .

What is the visual of my perfect life?

More notes. . .

How am I building meaningful relationships?

More notes. . .

What is the state of being I create by managing my thoughts?

More notes. . .

What opportunities exist for me to increase my financial wealth?

More notes. . .

What world exists that is beyond my imagination?

More notes. . .

I embrace the wholeness of life and the brilliance of all I am.

More notes. . .

How am I ready to evolve and accelerate?

More notes. . .

How do I feel when I see others receive abundance?

More notes. . .

When I have the courage to be ME how does my life unfold?

More notes. . .

How do I evolve through insight, harmony,
and connection?

More notes. . .

How do my dreams serve to align me with my inner gifts?

More notes. . .

How do I align with my perfect life?

More notes. . .

What would it take for me to receive more revenue?

More notes. . .

I allow myself to love and be loved.

More notes. . .

When I allow myself to be a conduit for abundance, prosperity, & health what shows up in my life?

More notes. . .

I am a living miracle.

More notes. . .

How do I align with my inner truth?

More notes. . .

As I think I vibrate: As I vibrate, I attract. What have I attracted through my vibration?

More notes. . .

I am a powerful abundance magnet.

More notes. . .

When do I show grace under pressure?

More notes. . .

How do I radiate success?

More notes. . .

How have the things I looked at changed
when I changed the way I looked at them?

More notes. . .

I will allow myself to PAUSE so everything
that is worthwhile can catch up with me.

More notes. . .

When I move beyond my limits what will I grow into?

More notes. . .

What my fear makes solid turns to mist
when I embrace it.

More notes. . .

What am I co-creating for my life?

More notes. . .

I am powerful beyond measure.

More notes. . .

All possibilities exist NOW! Which ones am I ready to embrace?

More notes. . .

I ask the Universe and I allow myself to receive.

More notes. . .

How am I building a powerful foundation for abundance?

More notes. . .

I am Source's divine plan.

More notes. . .

When I invite myself to evolve what shows
up in my life?

More notes. . .

I thrive in financial wellness.

More notes. . .

How do I stand as an influencer & new era conscious thought leader?

More notes. . .

As a vibrational influencer what do I stand for?

More notes. . .

My life is rich in infinite ways. What are 5 examples of this in my life?

More notes. . .

My mind and heart work together to create
a loving vibration.

More notes. . .

When I open my mind to possibilities and opportunities what will manifest in my life?

More notes. . .

Why have I chosen a fun and creative path
to abundance?

More notes. . .

PROSPERITY POWER PACK

1. *Nighttime Nuggets of Prosperity*
2. *Magical Morning Moments for Manifestation*
3. *Feeding Faith with Fantasy*

All books by Brenda Lynn Jacobson are available on her Amazon Author's Page

https://www.amazon.com/author/brenda.jacobson

MAGICAL MORNING MOMENTS for MANIFESTATION

Starting Each Day with Creating Abundance

Deep within you lives the power to manifest an abundance of anything you desire—**it is your birthright**. The key is to be vibrationally aligned to start manifesting from a place of your *HIGHEST TRUTH!* The freshness of the morning is the perfect time to harness your conscious mind and ensure it's on a powerful track for the day ahead. This book offers a simple and effective technique for aligning your conscious and subconscious minds and accelerating manifestation.

. . .

OTHER PUBLICATIONS

Accelerating Financial Greatness for Business Leaders

Combining new world science and ancient wisdom to provide insights and exercises to optimize financial flow. In this new world, prosperity comes into balance with value—providing access to new and advanced resources. This publication will powerfully position you for greater profitability from the inside out.

Embrace Your Accelerated Awakening

This Action Planner is an essential tool for preparing to enter the upper dimensions. It provides clarity about your vision—and strategies for growing into this new energy. *You are the plan!* It's about you mastering your thoughts, your emotions, and your intentions. Each time you return to an experience you'll notice an evolution. You'll emerge fully engulfed in and embracing the brilliant energy of your new dimension.

Prepare for Your Accelerated Awakening

This Action Planner is an essential tool for you in preparing to enter the accelerated energy of the higher dimensions. It helps you evolve and accelerate into who you choose to be—and growing up into this new energy. You're now in charge and are now empowered to step up and take responsibility for your life and your world. *You're the plan! We're all the plan*! It's not only about the evolution of humanity—it's about you learning your mastery—mastering your thoughts, your emotions, and your intentions.

The Awakened Empath

Are you withholding your gifts from those in need? Many Empaths are, simply because they're stuck in emotions that contract their world. The world desperately needs all the wisdom held deep within each of you. It's now time to wake up and introduce yourself—in all your brilliance—to the world.

Take this conscious journey to enlightenment and discover opportunities beyond your imagination.

Awakening Consciously

Paperback and eBook formats available on Amazon

Join the journey through your chakra system and discover how this ancient wisdom brings new relevance to life in the 21st century. As you discover the immensity of the system in which you're embedded, you identify with your universal connection, you open to receive guidance from your higher self and Universal Sources, and you realize you're part of the entire web of life. This realization enables you to embrace the wholeness of life and the brilliance of all that is—AND ALL THAT YOU ARE.

The Basics of Harnessing Your Chakra Power for Empaths

It's now time to take the next step in the evolutionary process and embrace your energy body and chakra system—learning how to read the signals, operate and maintain it in the most optimal way. This's by far the most impactful strategy for balancing and optimizing every aspect of your life. Through this awakening, you create a life based on a new level of energy, joy, and peace.

Harnessing Your Root Chakra Power

This's the second book in the *Harnessing Your Chakra Power series*. Congratulations on levelling up! In this Meditation Journey Through the Root Chakra—Intentional Journal you'll be introduced to a unique meditation called "*Into the Pause*". This'll awaken the Root chakra, ground you to the energy of the earth, and create a powerful foundation for all you desire. ALIGN & ALLOW.

Harnessing Your Sacral Chakra Power

This's the third book in the *Harnessing Your Chakra Power* series. Congratulations on elevating your game! In this Meditation Journey Through the Sacral Chakra—Intentional Journal you'll be introduced to a unique meditation helping you tap into the power of the Sacral chakra. Where you created a powerful container in the Root chakra you now generate dynamic flow of abundance to fill it up. CLEAR & CREATE

Harnessing Your Solar Plexus Chakra Power

This is the fourth book in the *Harnessing Your Chakra Power series*. Congratulations on moving on up the ladder of seven! In this Meditation Journey Through the Solar Plexus Chakra—Intentional Journal you'll tap into the power of the Solar Plexus chakra and reclaim your personal sovereignty. Having established a solid ground in the root chakra and a natural flow of emotions and movement in the sacral chakra, it's time to convert energy into action and POWER UP!

Harnessing Your Heart Chakra Power

This's the fifth book in the *Harnessing Your Chakra Power series*. In this Meditation Journey Through the Heart Chakra—Intentional Journal you'll be introduced to a unique meditation to tap into the power of the Heart chakra where you're introduced to the healing center of the energy body. This's the bridge between the upper and lower chakra systems—the space for you to create balance between giving and receiving, loving, and being loved.

Harnessing Your Throat Chakra Power

The sixth book in the *Harnessing Your Chakra Power series*. In this Meditation Journey Through the Throat Chakra—Intentional Journal you'll take the first step into the realm of the spiritual chakras and discover the voice of your soul. In the first four chakras, you focused on movement, activity, and relationships. In the fifth your attention moves to communication as you connect your newly discovered and revitalized self with the outside world.

Harnessing Your Third Eye Chakra Power

In this seventh book of the *Harnessing Your Chakra Power series* you'll discover a world beyond imagination. This Meditation Journey Through the Third Eye Chakra—Intentional Journal will open your mind to see and understand. As you enter the head, you move beyond the physical world of time and space and into the symbolic realm of the mind. You honor your spiritual connection and expand your spiritual language.

Harnessing Your Crown Chakra Power

Welcome to the Age of Consciousness! This's the final book in the *Harnessing Your Chakra Power series*. In this Meditation Journey Through the Crown Chakra—Intentional Journal you'll open the crown chakra. This's not as much about increasing your own consciousness, as it is about expanding to merge with the Universal consciousness. You provide a healthy foundation for the seventh chakra by keeping your mind open to new knowledge.

30-Day Wake Up Call

With the rapidity of change we're currently facing, people find themselves waking up. This doesn't need to be difficult or take much time. In this Mini Course and Workbook, you'll experience gentle shifts in habits and behaviors that only take a few minutes a day. This 30-Day Wake-Up Call is an invitation for you to begin your awakening journey and transform your life.

Getting to the Root of Your Financial Greatness for Empaths

Many things must change for Empaths be compensated appropriately for the gifts they bring to the world. They need to tap into the deep truth that lives within them and align with the brilliant new way of flourishing in this world. The insights and self-reflection in this book will elevate you to the upper realm of reality and get you to the Root of Your Financial Greatness.

We Believe Together We Can Create a Fabulous New World!

"Happiness is when what you think, what you say and what you do are in harmony."—Mahatma Gandhi

ABOUT BRENDA LYNN

After falling 3,000 feet down a mountain while skiing, I spent over five years recovering. This took me *into a pause*. The first year was consumed by my body disintegrating and the next four were invested in rebuilding every aspect of my life—physical, emotional, mental, and spiritual. My body healed in about two years however my emotions kept me stuck for another two.

This was a hidden gift as I experienced the power of sitting still and exploring what was buried deep within myself. I became intimately connected to my body, mind, emotions, and my higher self. Divine guidance came on very strong offering me a lifeline.

As I witnessed the events of 2020—the pandemic, the shutdown of the world and the bold and subtle side effects—I realized the world had gone *Into a Pause*, much as I had after my accident. This's a time to settle the frenetic energy, to reconnect to our bodies, our passions—*OUR TRUTH*. It's a time of great opportunity—only if we tap into the abundance of resources at our disposal

This experience combined with 25 years as a finance executive and business strategist, bestselling author, international speaker and trainer, exposed me to numerous strategies and techniques that contribute to personal performance. I'm passionate about helping people consciously create their experience and build the life of their dreams.

- I believe TOGETHER we can create a new world.
- I believe in GOOSEBUMPS.
- I believe each of us has the potential for MAGIC.
- I believe in subtle MESSAGES from our bodies.
- I believe EMOTIONS are our guidance system.
- I believe THOUGHTS create our world.

CONTACT BRENDA LYNN

I would enjoy hearing about your experience with *Language of Emotions* and I welcome you into this community. You can contact me through the website at

AwakeningConsciously.com/contact

This site includes many other resources for you to Awaken Consciously and join us in *creating a new world*.

Check out the abundance of courses offered on Gumroad at

https://brendalynnleadership.gumroad.com/

To explore other resources please follow/connect with me in other parts of my social media multiverse by joining me on Linktr.ee.

https://linktr.ee/brendalynnleaders.

Printed in Great Britain
by Amazon